Mother's Little Helper

Twelve Heart-to-Heart Talks of a Mother to Her Daughter

2915 Forest Avenue | Kansas City, MO 64109

Nihil Obstat
Rev. John J. Clifford, S.J.
Censor Dept.
July 29, 1952

Imprimatur
† Samuel Cardinal Stritch
Archbishop of Chicago
July 30, 1952

Cover image by Petra Eschenlohr

ANGELUS PRESS
2915 FOREST AVENUE
KANSAS CITY, MISSOURI 64109
PHONE (816) 753-3150
FAX (816) 753-3557
ORDER LINE 1-800-966-7337
www.angeluspress.org

ISBN: 978-1-892331-45-8
Revised Edition: February 2007
Revised Edition, Fourth Printing: November 2018

Printed in the United States of America

This Little Work
is placed under the gracious patronage
of
THE IMMACULATE MOTHER
and lovingly dedicated to
A. and D.H.,
for whom it was originally written

Contents

Foreword. 1

Part One:
To be discussed with girls ages 9-12
Instruction 1 8
Instruction 2 12
Instruction 3 16
Instruction 4 20

Part Two:
To be discussed with girls ages 12-14
Instruction 5 26
Instruction 6 32
Instruction 7 37
Instruction 8 44

Part Three:
To be discussed with young women ages 14-16
Instruction 9 52
Instruction 10 56
Instruction 11 61
Instruction 12 68

Foreword

Though Catholic educators are agreed that it is the duty of a mother to give her growing daughters timely instruction on what are called the facts of life, mothers may still be found who either neglect this duty or perform it in a very imperfect manner. One reason for this neglect, no doubt, is the tendency to shift most of the responsibility for the child's training to the Church and the school, despite the fact that the parents, and especially the mother, are the child's chief educators and the most efficient of all schools is a truly Christian home. Yet probably the most common reason why even some conscientious mothers fail in this particular duty is that they realize the extreme delicacy of the task and simply do not know how to go about it.

It is hoped that the present little work will prove to be just what such mothers want—a little helper in the difficult task of instructing and training their growing daughters, since it places on the mother's lips the exact words to use in imparting the necessary information. There is the more reason for this hope inasmuch as these instructions have actually been used by a mother over a period of years, with most satisfactory results, in instructing her two daughters; and many other women who were permitted to read them—single women and mothers as well as nuns—have expressed the wish that they would soon be published and made available for the use of mothers everywhere.

It should be carefully noted, however, that the purpose of publishing these instructions is not to relieve the mother of her task but to help her in fulfilling it; and, therefore, that they are not intended to be given to a girl to read but to be discussed with her by her mother. The very delicacy and seriousness of the information contained in these instructions require that it be imparted under favorable circumstances and with proper precautions; and no situation could be more propitious for the purpose than a heart-to-heart chat between mother and daughter. It is precisely the building up of a loving mutual understanding between mother and daughter that is so necessary for the proper guidance of the latter during the years of adolescence; and nothing contributes more to this understanding than the mother's readiness to lend a willing ear to her daughter's problems and an equal readiness on the part of the daughter to place her entire confidence in her mother.

To further this desirable end, the mother should discuss these instructions with each daughter separately in a private interview at which there will be ample opportunity for reviewing certain issues, clarifying anything obscure, and answering questions. Yet, though permitted to ask questions, the daughter should also be made to understand that she must restrain inordinate curiosity. Hence, if her mother defers the answers to certain questions, she must be content and trust her mother implicitly to give her all the information that will be useful to her in due time.

It may seem to some that the information imparted in this little booklet, and especially in Part One of it, is inadequate, and that the girl of twelve or thirteen might just as well be told the whole truth with all details. It may be true, indeed, that many, possibly even most, girls of sixteen in our day have acquired more information about sex than is given in this entire treatise. Yet it is more than likely that the reason why they obtained so much information (usually from all kinds of improper sources) was that their mothers did not instruct them and, by gradually satisfying their legitimate curiosity and retaining their confidence, did not preclude the uneasy desire to find out more.

At all events, the mother who used these instructions found them to be perfectly adequate for her two daughters. Though living in a large city, attending a large school, and leading the normal life of other girls, her daughters never sought nor obtained information from other sources, because they knew that their mother would give it to them in due time.

The chief reason, however, why so little biological information was included in this work is that it seemed desirable to keep the subject on as high a plane as possible; and that could not be done by approaching the subject from a biological or botanical angle, as if man were merely a somewhat more perfect animal and not rather just a little below the angels. Only by constantly referring to the fact that man is the work of God, and that every detail of his origin and development has been ordained by God's infinite wisdom, can one succeed in making the child realize that God alone is the author and master of life and therefore that all the processes of life are as sacred as they are mysterious and admirable.

Unless a girl acquires the supernatural attitude toward this subject right in the beginning, there will be danger of her having a wrong attitude toward it all through life. But if the subject is introduced and unfolded to her by her own mother in a delicate and reverent manner, with constant reference to God and a minimum of physical details, the first impression she receives will be sacred, deep, and lasting; and she will then be well prepared to acquire more detailed information from other Catholic sources when her age or circumstances require it.

The age at which the first instruction may best be read to individual girls, as well as how long an interval should elapse before the reading of each successive instruction, will naturally depend upon the type of girl and each one's peculiar circumstances. Experience proves that too early initiation into the mysteries of life does not make a child truly wise, but produces rather that unlovely and preposterous thing—the sophisticated child.

As a rule, the first three instructions should be given before puberty, or, at the latest, at puberty. The remaining ones can easily be distributed over a period of five or six years, at longer or shorter intervals, according as a prudent mother deems it most advisable. All the instructions, also those found in Part Three, should be discussed by the mother with her daughter and not simply given to her to read; because this practice will foster that feeling of filial confidence in her mother that is so important to a girl.

Important as it is, especially in this enlightened and irreverent age, to arm girls in due time with a sufficient knowledge of the facts of life, it cannot be overemphasized that knowledge alone will never suffice to prevent moral lapses. Far more important, then, for the mother than the task of instructing her daughter, is the task of helping her to develop a strong Christian character by gently yet firmly training her to control her passions, to avoid dangerous occasions of sin, and to make constant use of the supernatural aids of the sacraments and prayer. This must be done from childhood on, yes, from very infancy on; and the main part of this task should be accomplished before the task of imparting the truths contained in this booklet is begun.

From what has been said, it should be evident that these instructions are not intended to be placed in pamphlets racks or sold to the general public, but entrusted only to parents, priests, and other mature persons endowed with the necessary prudence to use them according to the author's intentions.

Part One

To be discussed with girls
ages 9-12 years

Instruction 1

My dear Daughter,

One of the very first things you learned in Catechism class was the answer to the question: "Who made you?" You were taught that God made you; that He made heaven and earth, the land and the sea, plants and animals, and all things. Later on you were told *how* God made the first man and the first woman. The first man, Adam, God made by making a body of the slime of the earth and breathing into it an immortal soul. And Eve, the first woman, God made out of a rib which He took from Adam's side while he was asleep.

You were never told how God made all other men and women; but you know that they must be made in a different way than Adam and Eve, because God made Adam at once a full-grown man and Eve a full-grown woman; and all other men and women came into the world as babies.

Now, have you never wondered how God makes babies, and where they came from? Perhaps at some point you asked me where babies come from. I told you that they come from God, which is true. But things come from God in different ways.

You see, my dear, when we say that God made all things, or that He is the Creator of all things, we do not mean that He made everything directly out of nothing. God made the peaches and the apples, which you like to eat, and the roses, which you love to see; but you know that they are not made directly out of nothing, because you have seen them growing on trees or bushes. At first the peach tree produced buds; the buds grew into blossoms, and the blossoms into peaches. And even the tree itself was not made out of nothing; because you know very well that trees, like plants and flowers, grow up out of seeds. Yet it is entirely correct to say that God made them; because in the beginning, thousands of years ago, God created the first trees and plants and flowers and made them so that each one would produce seed from which other trees and plants would develop.

Thus God is the Creator of all things, since He made everything, either directly out of nothing, or indirectly by making certain things produce other things of the same kind. This shows the greatness of God's power. Men can make flowers, too, that is, artificial ones; and they can make them so perfect that you can hardly distinguish them from natural ones. But no man can make a flower that will grow and have seed and produce other flowers.

This is all very interesting to you, I am sure; but the most interesting thing is how God makes man. Every day thousands of new children come into the world. Do they just drop into their cradles out of the air like the lovely snowflakes that fall from the sky? Or do their Guardian Angels bring them down from heaven and place them in the arms of their mothers? No. God could create them in that way, if He wanted to, but He doesn't. There are hundreds of ways in which God could bring children into the world; but He chose only one way: and since He is infinitely wise and holy, the way He chose must surely be the best. But what is that way? When God creates a new human being, instead of making its body, as He did Adam's out of the slime of the earth, He makes it out of a substance which He prepares in the body of its mother. In the very same instant that the tiny body is formed, God makes an immortal soul directly out of nothing, and unites it to the body, which is then nourished and developed inside its mother's body until the time comes for it to be born.

It was in this way that the Son of God Himself became man, as you can see from the Gospel that is read on the feast of the Annunciation. "The Angel Gabriel," so we read there, "was sent by God into a city of Galilee called Nazareth to a virgin espoused to a man whose name was Joseph, of the house of David. And the virgin's name was Mary. And the Angel being come in, said to her: 'Hail, full of grace, the Lord is with thee. Blessed art thou among women....Behold, thou shalt conceive in thy womb and shalt bring forth a son, and thou shalt call His name Jesus. He shall be great and shall be called the Son of the Most High....' And Mary said: 'Behold the handmaid of the Lord: be it done to me according to thy word.'"

As soon as Mary uttered these words, she conceived by the Holy Ghost, as we say in the Angelus; that means: by the action of the Holy Ghost, the body and soul of Jesus were made in Mary's womb and united to the Second Person of the Blessed Trinity. So you see that the sublime mystery of the Incarnation of the Son of God was accomplished in the chaste womb of the immaculate virgin Mary. The womb, you must know, is that wonderful organ inside a woman's body in which a child is conceived, that is, brought into existence, then nourished, just as its mother is nourished by the food she takes, and from which it is finally brought forth or born and then nourished at its mother's breast. And as Jesus was formed in the womb of His blessed Mother, so every child that comes into the world was also formed in its mother's womb.

So now you know how God creates little children; and you can now understand, too, why a mother loves her child so much; since the child's body was formed out of her own substance and fed with milk at its mother's breast. But now listen, my dear. You were never told about this before, because the creation of a child is something so wonderful that a girl is usually not told about it until she is old enough to appreciate it. Then, too, it is a very mysterious and sacred subject which girls should not talk about among themselves. You are now old enough and wise enough to keep this information to yourself and to speak about it with no one but me. As time goes on, I will tell you more about these things and other subjects; and you should not hesitate to ask me any questions that come to your mind. I know you and I love you; therefore trust me absolutely, and I will tell you all that you should know at the proper time.

Instruction 2

My dear Daughter,

In the instruction I gave you some time ago, I explained to you that our Lord was conceived in His Blessed Mother's womb on the day of the Annunciation. From that day until He was born, Jesus lay hidden away beneath His Mother's heart. If you recall how happy you were the first time you received Jesus in Holy Communion, you can imagine how much greater must have been the joy that Mary felt. For when you receive Jesus in Holy Communion, He remains with you only a short time; but He remained with Mary for nine months, so that during all that time Mary knew that, no matter where she went or what she did, whether working or praying, waking or sleeping, she had little Jesus within Her.

As the Incarnation took place on March 25, you will now understand why the birth or the Nativity of our Lord is celebrated on December 25–just nine months later. Nine months is the usual time that elapses between the conception and the birth of a child, and during that time the mother is said to be "with child" or to be an expectant mother. As the Blessed Virgin knew by the annunciation of the angel the exact day that Jesus was conceived, she also knew when He was to be born, and she accordingly took with her the necessary infant clothing when she had to journey to Bethlehem. Other women are not so fortunate as to know at once when God has given them a child; but after a few weeks it is indicated by certain physical signs, and they can then figure out approximately when the child will be born.

It is to these facts of nature that the evangelist St. Luke refers when he says in the Gospel of the first Mass on Christmas Day: "And Joseph also went up from Galilee... to Bethlehem to be enrolled with Mary his espoused wife, who was with child. And it came to pass that when they were there, her days were accomplished that she should be delivered. And she brought forth her first-born son and wrapped him up in swaddling clothes and laid him in a manger."

As Mary carried Jesus under her heart for nine months, so Mary, too, had been carried in like manner for the same length of time by St. Ann. You will find, therefore, if you count the months, that also exactly nine months elapsed between the Immaculate Conception of the Blessed Virgin and her Nativity, since the former is celebrated on December 8, and the latter on September 8. It may be well to remind you here what is meant by the Immaculate Conception. When other children are conceived, their souls are stained with original sin; but because God created Mary's soul in the state of sanctifying grace, we say that she was conceived without sin, or that her Conception was immaculate. It was to honor the great privilege of Mary's Immaculate Conception that the Church attached an indulgence of three hundred days to the little prayer: "O Mary, conceived without sin, pray for us who have recourse to thee."

Since you learned about the origin of children, perhaps the thought has come to you: but I wonder how it comes that only married women have children? There are several things that must be told you in answer to that question, but the most important thing is this. Bringing up children, taking proper care of them, obtaining food and shelter for them, training and instructing them is by no means an easy task. For this reason, and no doubt for other wise reasons, God in His infinite wisdom and fatherly care for His children, ordained that every child should have also a father, who should love it, labor for the support of both mother and child, provide a home for them, and form with them that society that we call the family. And that the parents might not separate and deprive the child of the loving care that it needs, God also ordained that the parents must be united in marriage and be bound by the marriage contract to live together until separated by death.

Another thing that you may have wondered about is why a doctor is usually called when a baby is born. You may even have heard people say: "The doctor brought us a new baby." This does not mean that the doctor brought the baby into the house, but that he helped the mother to bring it into the world. You see, my dear, a mother usually suffers great pain and sometimes has great difficulty in giving birth to a child, and a new born baby is a very delicate creature; and for that reason it is advisable and sometimes even necessary to have a doctor to assist the mother and give her and her infant the best of care. That is why it is very common nowadays for women to go to a hospital when they expect the birth of a child. If Adam and Eve had not sinned, giving birth to a child would have been easy and painless; but in punishment for their sin, God addressed to Eve the words: "In sorrow shalt thou bring forth children." And that is also what our Lord referred to when He said to His apostles in the Gospel that is read on the third Sunday after Easter: "A woman when she is in labor, hath sorrow because her hour is come; but when she hath brought forth the child, she remembereth no more the anguish for joy that a man is born into the world."

Instruction 3

My dear Daughter,

Even when you were still a little child you noticed the difference between persons of different ages. You noticed that some were mere babies; others were children; others, young men and young women; and still others were grown-up and elderly men and women. It did not take long for you to realize that the difference in these various persons was due to age and growth; and so you soon began to speak about your own growing up and what you would do or be when you were grown-up or when you "got big."

Well, my child, the process of your growing up has been going on now without ceasing since you were a baby; and you are gradually becoming aware that, as you grew from a baby into a young girl, you are now growing from a young girl into a young woman. What you probably did not know heretofore, is the fact that growth or growing up does not consist merely in getting taller and bigger, but in certain other changes that take place in the interior and exterior organs of your body. Just as a tree that grows up from seed, for example, an orange tree, not only gets larger but develops or puts forth branches and then blossoms, and finally yields fruit: so also your body goes through a long course of development, during which certain organs begin to function, *i.e.*, become active, that were formerly inactive; and certain substances are gradually produced that did not exist in you before.

Among the most important of these changes is the one that takes place in a girl when she is developing from a girl into a woman. It is, in fact, the change that marks the time when a girl has become a woman or, as is said, has reached maturity. You remember my having told you that God makes the body of a child out of a substance in the body of its mother. This substance is not found in your body so long as you are a mere girl, because the organs that produce it are not yet active. The age at which these organs first begin to function varies in different girls, as not all girls develop at the same rate. In many girls they begin to function at the age of twelve or thirteen; in some, already at eleven; and in others again as late even as sixteen or seventeen.

When these organs do begin to function and to produce that precious substance, since God does not always make use of it for the formation of a child and nature supplies it in abundance, the unused portion, together with a quantity of blood, passes from the body at regular intervals. This is what is known as menstruation; and once it has begun, it usually occurs every four weeks, or thirteen times in the course of a whole year.

As menstruation is a perfectly natural function, which all normal women experience from the dawn of womanhood until they are about forty-five years of age, it is important for you to understand right from the start what to think of it and how to act in regard to it. Understand well, then, my child, that menstruation is not a sickness or a disorder, but the natural effect of the activity of those organs that are common to all women. If those organs are inactive, it is impossible for a woman to become a mother. So if it is a little disagreeable at times, do not be put out about it; but think it is a necessary requirement for the dignity of motherhood, and that if all other women have to put up with it, you will gladly endure it too.

Therefore make no attempt to stop the flow, because you cannot stop it anyhow; and if you could succeed in stopping it, it would only do you harm. But while you cannot stop it, you may and you should do all that is necessary for the sake of health and cleanliness while it lasts. Your body being a temple of the Holy Ghost, not only due regard for health, but even proper reverence for God's temple requires that you try to keep it sweet and clean. For this reason you should bathe your entire body quite regularly, washing even those parts about which you feel the greatest delicacy and reserve in the same matter-of-fact way as your face and hands. The latter precaution is especially necessary at the time of your monthly periods. At that time, lukewarm water is recommended as best for washing the parts mentioned, although at other times moderately cold water is to be preferred. At no time, however, should really hot water be used for that purpose.

Regular and timely attention to cleanliness will go far towards preventing itching in those delicate parts. But should you be troubled with itching there nevertheless, you must know that there is nothing wrong in touching yourself to stop the itching, just as you sometimes rub even so delicate an organ as the ball of your eye. You should be very careful, however, never to touch those parts for the sake of any pleasure you might find in doing so, as that would not only be sinful, but could even result in serious injury to the inner or outer organs. Hence, if the itching is only slight, it is advisable simply to ignore it, as it will probably disappear of itself.

Now that you know the meaning of menstruation, you will not be alarmed when it occurs, but will realize that it has given you a new dignity—the dignity of being able to be used by God for the creation of new human beings. When you notice it for the first time, tell me right away, and I will teach you how to take care of yourself. In the meantime, do not be anxious whether it will occur soon or only after several more months or years; and until it happens, try to put all curiosity concerning it out of your mind. Then when it does set in, bear it patiently like a little woman. Do not be like some girls who are vexed by what they call the mess of it, and who declare that they wish they were boys. Rather be glad that you are what God made you. And remember that whatever disagreeableness there may be about this function is due to the sin of Mother Eve, and that you have to endure only what St. Cecilia, St. Catherine, St. Elizabeth, St. Ann and all other saintly women, including the Mother of God herself, had to endure before you.

Instruction 4

My dear Daughter,

When I told you that God creates children within their mother's body, I said that God wanted only married women to have babies so that the children would have both a father and a mother to love them and to take care of them. It does not follow from that, however, that all married women have children. Some women are married for years without having any, although they would dearly love to have children. Thus St. Ann, the wife of St. Joachim, had no child until she was quite old, when she became the mother of the Blessed Virgin. Just why this is, no one fully understands; but usually there is some physical cause, just as there is some hidden physical cause why some people remain small and others grow tall; some get stout and some stay lean.

In some cases, however, married women have no children because they do not do what is necessary in order to have a child. You see, dear, because the parents have to take care of their children and must often work hard to be able to feed, clothe, and shelter them, God wants the parents to give their consent to having children by doing what He has ordained that they should do if they want to have children. Consequently, if the parents agree not to do that, they will never have any children.

Then, another reason why God wants the parents to co-operate with Him in the creation of new human beings, is that He wants the parents to have a great love for their children; and everybody naturally loves what he himself helped to make. Thus a girl is much attached to a piece of fancy work or a painting that she made herself. And if she worked long and hard at such a thing out of love for her parents in order to make them a gift of it, we say that it was a work of love.

Now, God in His infinite wisdom wanted every child to be also a work of love–the result of the love of husband and wife for each other. For this reason He has made it natural for certain men and women to love each other more than any other person, or, as we say, to fall in love with each other, and then to get married by promising to live together and to love each other until death. Since the child is formed of the mother's own substance, as I have already told you, in a little nest, as it were, which God has prepared beneath every woman's heart, it is only natural that a mother loves her child very much. But God wanted the father also to have a great love for his children; and therefore God has given the father also a share in bringing the child into existence. The father can just as truly say: "This is my child," as the mother; for without the father, the child could not have come into being. The only child who never had a real human father was our dear Lord Himself. God worked a special miracle to create His human body in the womb of the Blessed Virgin; and that is why St. Joseph is called only the foster father of Jesus.

But what does the father's share in bringing the child into existence consist in? It consists in an act of love. You know, my dear, that a kiss is an act of love. And because God wants husband and wife to love each other more than anyone else, it is always natural and proper for them to show their love by kissing. But the most intimate act of love is embracing; and it is by a very intimate embrace of his wife that a husband makes it possible for her to become a mother.

You see then, dearest, how wonderfully and beautifully God has arranged everything for the creation of a child. He wants every child to be the result of the love that its father and mother have for each other.

Yet, holy and sacred as is this embrace in the married state, it is not lawful for unmarried persons. Even kisses between young men and young women are often sinful because they might lead to this embrace; but the intimate embrace itself of husband and wife would always be a mortal sin for unmarried persons. You can easily understand what a difference marriage makes, if you recall what difference the Sacrament of Holy Orders makes. A priest is a human being just as well as a layman; yet because the priest has received Holy Orders, it is a holy and sacred thing for him to touch and handle the Sacred Host, while for an unordained person, the same act would be a mortal sin and a sacrilege.

Still, since it is possible for an unmarried girl to allow a man to give her the marital embrace, it is possible also for an unmarried girl to become a mother. But, as I said, in that case the marital embrace would be a grievous sin for the girl as well as for the boy. It would be no sin, of course, for the girl, if a man would overpower her and give her that embrace entirely against her will; though such a thing does not easily happen, as the girl would at once know he was doing something wrong and could offer resistance. Still, because of the possibility, a girl should beware of being all alone with a man in a place where they could not be seen by others; *e.g.*, in a car parked in a dark place.

Now I have told you enough of this wonderful mystery for the present. Later on, when necessary, I will tell you more. From what I have said, you will understand that, although St. Joseph was really Mary's husband, he never gave her the marital embrace, because God wanted Jesus to be made in a miraculous manner and to have no earthly father but only His Father in heaven.

Here let me warn you again not to talk about these things with other girls; and if they begin to do so, talk of something else or go away. As I told you in the beginning, this is a sacred subject, and young girls are too giddy to speak of it with proper reverence. Besides, you still do not know enough about it, and if you speak of it with them, you may give them wrong ideas or get wrong ideas from them. All through life, we have to control our curiosity in regard to some things; so learn to control your curiosity about this matter for the love of God. Remember what happened to Eve for being over curious and for getting information from the wrong source. So whenever you want any information on this subject, ask me, and I will tell you all that will be useful for you at the time.

Part Two

To be discussed with girls
ages 12-14

Instruction 5

My dear Daughter,

In far off China, even until recently, pagan mothers often cared so little for their children that they would put a new-born child out on the street to die; but that, if they were paid a small sum of money, they would allow Christian missionaries to take the child and baptize it and bring it up a Christian. The cruelty of those Chinese mothers certainly seemed very strange and very sad to you. Yet, as they lived so far away and you knew that they were pagans, you no doubt thought that the destruction of infant lives was something very exceptional in the affairs of human life, and you probably have had that same opinion up to the present time.

I wish it were possible, my dear child, to leave you under that impression always. You will grow up and will have to act your part on the stage of life. And as life is a serious business, you must be instructed how to act. You must be told what you have to expect, so that you will not be taken by surprise and in your confusion make serious mistakes.

Since, therefore, you are developing rapidly and will soon be a real young lady, it is now time for you to be told that terrible wickedness is found not only in far distant countries or in the histories of ancient nations, but right here in your own country; yes, even in your own city, and perhaps even among your very neighbors and acquaintances. Probably you gasp at the idea and think it almost impossible; yet it is only too true that hundreds of thousands of babies are killed in this country every year.

This shows how wicked people can become when they do not listen to the teachings of religion. If a human life gets in the way of their desire for ease, comfort, or pleasure, and they can do away with it without being punished by law, they simply do away with it. In this instruction, then, I want to speak to you about the sacredness of human life, so that you will understand better what an awful crime it is to destroy it. It is true, the willful killing of an adult person or even of a child in cold blood is regarded with horror by all civilized peoples. But many people do not consider it so serious a thing to destroy the life of an unborn child; and it was chiefly of unborn children that I was speaking, when I said that many children are killed every year.

Probably the main reason why many people do not think it a serious matter to destroy the life of an unborn child is the fact that the child is not fully developed and has never been seen and in consequence is not missed. Then, too, since in the early months of its life before birth, a child can often be got rid of very easily–merely by means of certain drugs or medicines, a woman who does not want to bother with a baby thinks it a very simple thing to take a little medicine and get rid of it, that is, murder it. I say murder; for no matter how innocent the taking of medicine may seem to be, to take it for the purpose of destroying the life of an unborn child is nothing less than willful murder; just as much as it would be to give deadly poison to a child already born.

You see, my dear child, from the very first moment that God creates a soul and unites it to a body in the mother's womb, that tiny creature (smaller at first than a sparkling dewdrop) is a real human being–a being endowed with an understanding and free will, a being that will exist for all eternity. And since it is a human being, it has a strict right to its life, just as truly as the aged man or hopeless invalid who is no longer able to take care of himself; and therefore it has also a strict right to the nourishment and care it needs in order to live and grow and be born. And not only the child has a right to its life which no one can dispute; but, more so still, God has a right to its life, which no one can violate without committing a grievous sin.

When God created man, He gave him power over the lives of irrational animals; but the power over the lives of his fellowmen God reserved to Himself. Consequently, when amid thunder and lightning on Mount Sinai, God solemnly declared, "Thou shalt not kill," He forbade the killing of every human being, whether old or young, sick or well, born or unborn, except in a few cases where it is permitted in self-defense, in a just war, or by lawful authority for the punishment of a serious crime.

You can understand now that, if it is a great wrong for a pagan mother to expose her newborn babe to almost certain death, it must be a far greater crime for a Catholic woman to kill her unborn child. For the pagan mother knows nothing of the necessity of Baptism; but a Catholic mother knows that by killing the child in her womb, she prevents it from being baptized and from ever going to heaven. You should know that unbaptized babies go to a place called limbo. These unborn children did not commit sins through their own fault so as to deserve hell or purgatory, but on the other hand, they never received baptism to wash away original sin. These babies go to a place of natural happiness but without the blissful look at God which is called the beatific vision.

God created the soul of that child for the eternal happiness of heaven; Jesus died on the cross that He might wash original sin from its soul with His Precious Blood; and the Holy Ghost wished to clothe it with the beautiful white robe of sanctifying grace. If, in spite of knowing all this, a Catholic mother deliberately does something that keeps her child from obtaining all those blessings, she just as much as says: "I don't care if God did create this child for heaven, or if Jesus did die for it, or if the Holy Ghost does want to sanctify it. I don't want to be bothered with it, and so I'll get rid of it." Isn't it awful? You probably still doubt whether a Catholic mother can really be so heartless; but it is a sad fact that some of them sometimes are.

I must add here as a partial excuse for some women that are guilty of this sin, especially non-Catholic women, that they have never been properly instructed on this matter; and, therefore, although their own conscience should tell them and does tell them that it is wrong, still it does not appear to them to be as terrible a crime as it really is. And very often, too, they are told by other women that it is the proper thing to do, if they are poor or if they already have several children to take care of.

The sin of willfully causing the death of an unborn child is called abortion. If its death is caused without any fault of the mother by being accidentally ejected from the womb, this is called a miscarriage and is not a sin. Another expression that you may come across sometime is "birth control" or "birth prevention," which is another grievously sinful way of keeping from having children. The fact that you sometimes find these expressions in Catholic papers is another reason why it seemed advisable to give you this information at the present time. You know now why Catholic editors condemn it and why Catholic priests preach against it.

But suppose a mother were extremely poor and already had a large family, would it be wrong for her also to practice abortion or birth control? Yes, my child, even then it would be a grievous sin. You must remember that no mother can have a child unless God gives it to her; and if God wants her to have a child, it is His holy will that she accept it and bring it up for heaven. Very often it is the last child that is the source of the greatest joy and consolation to its parents. St. Theresa of the Child Jesus was her parents' ninth and last child; St. Ignatius of Loyola, the thirteenth.

Young as you are, I am sure you realize that this instruction has added a most serious and important piece of information to your growing stock of knowledge. And now that you have learned at the very beginning of your young womanhood that birth prevention is an awful crime, I am confident that you will always have the greatest horror of it, no matter how many people practice it, and no matter what they say to defend it.

Beware, however, my child, of suspecting that because certain married women have only one or two or no children, they must be guilty of this sin. There are so many innocent reasons why a woman may remain childless, that we have no right to judge anyone guilty of this sin unless she herself has admitted it.

Instruction 6

My dear Daughter,

Though you may not have given much attention to the fact, you have undoubtedly heard or read at some time that it was an extraordinary privilege for the Blessed Virgin to be at the same time a virgin and a mother. She is, in fact, the only woman that ever became a mother without ceasing to be a virgin. If you have thought about the matter at all, probably you thought that a virgin is the same as an unmarried woman, and that as soon as a virgin marries she is no longer a virgin. That is not correct. A virgin does not cease to be a virgin by the mere fact that she contracts a valid marriage, but by the fact that she and her husband make use of the marriage right, *i.e.*, the right to the marital embrace conferred by the Sacrament of Matrimony. And as most married couples do that soon after being married, married women are no longer classed as virgins but as matrons.

Now, from what I told you in a previous instruction, you know that no woman can conceive a child naturally or become what is called an expectant mother without the co-operation of the child's father. Hence, when Mary had given birth to Jesus, her friends and relatives took it for granted that she had become a mother through the co-operation of St. Joseph in the same natural way as every other mother. Even the Blessed Virgin herself had no idea how she could become a mother in any other way when the angel appeared to her and declared that she would conceive in her womb and bring forth a son. Therefore she said to the angel: "How shall this be done, because I know not man?" By the words "I know not man," Mary meant that she did not make use of her marriage right to the marital embrace, because she had made the vow of perpetual virginity. The angel then explained to her that she would become the mother of Jesus in a supernatural manner by a special act of the Holy Ghost.

And just as Mary did not understand at first how she could remain a virgin and still become a mother, so neither did St. Joseph. When it became plain to St. Joseph, therefore, from Mary's changed appearance, that she was with child, and he knew full well that he was not the child's father, he decided to leave her; although the very thought of parting from so dear and holy a spouse almost broke his noble heart.

These extraordinary events and how God cleared up the doubts of St. Joseph are narrated by St. Matthew in the Gospel of the feast of St. Joseph in the following manner:

> Now the generation of Christ was in this wise. When as His mother Mary was espoused to Joseph, before they came together, she was found with child of the Holy Ghost. Whereupon Joseph, her husband, being a just man, and not willing publicly to expose her, was minded to put her away privately. But while he thought on these things, behold the angel of the Lord appeared to him in his sleep, saying: "Joseph, son of David, fear not to take unto thee Mary, thy wife; for that which is conceived in her is of the Holy Ghost. And she shall bring forth a son, and thou shalt call His name Jesus; for He shall save His people from their sins."

It is clear from this gospel narrative that for a virgin to conceive and become a mother is something so extraordinary that an angel of God had to come to St. Joseph to make it possible for him to believe it. If a wife permits another man, who is not her husband, to embrace her just as if he were her husband, she commits the sin that is called adultery. Now, as St. Joseph was sure that Mary was too holy to have committed even the least sin, he was at a loss how to explain her motherhood, until the angel brought him the happy tidings that she had become the mother of the Redeemer through a miracle wrought by the Holy Ghost.

Having mentioned the sin of adultery, it will be useful to add here a little further explanation. You know from your catechism that adultery is a sin against the sixth commandment or a sin of impurity; and it may seem odd to you that what is entirely lawful when done by a husband with his wife is a sin of impurity if done by the same husband with a woman who is not his wife. I have already explained why such a thing is sinful if done by unmarried persons; namely, because the Sacrament of Matrimony gives certain rights and duties that the unmarried do not have. But even married people have these rights and duties only in regard to their own partners in marriage and not in regard to other married persons. And the reason is this. It is the duty of the father to provide for his own child; but if a wife would consent to the marital embraces of another man besides her husband, she would not know which was the father of her children.

And now, my dear, I must warn you against a very serious mistake. You might suppose, as a certain girl did, because adultery is the sin of a married person, that the sixth commandment is only for the married, and that unmarried persons cannot commit sins of impurity. That would be a grave mistake. You must know, my dear child, that there are two kinds of chastity–virginal chastity, or the chastity of the unmarried; and conjugal chastity, or the chastity of the married; and a sin against either kind of chastity is called a sin of impurity. Certain kisses and embraces that are permitted only to husband and wife would be sins of impurity if done by others. Yet there are certain other actions that are *never* permitted to *anybody*, and are always sins of impurity, whether done by a married person or by a single person, whether alone or with another.

How I wish you would never need to know anything about this vice! But if you are to be kept from falling into the treacherous quicksand of impurity, you must be told where it is, or at least where you may remain and be sure that you are safe. For this reason, in the following instructions, I shall give you explanations and warnings that will be useful to you both at the present time and in the future for the preservation of the necessary and beautiful virtue of holy purity. But, as you cannot begin too soon, let me here give you a few general directions what to do and what to avoid in order to preserve and foster this beautiful virtue.

1. Avoid the occasions of sin. "He that loveth danger will perish in it." In particular avoid bad companions; sensational magazines, books, and papers; indecent and suggestive games and dances and other wild amusements.

2. Develop your will-power, which you will need to resist temptation, by avoiding idleness and effeminacy.

To this end, always keep yourself usefully occupied either with work or wholesome recreation (especially outdoors); accustom yourself to hard work, to disagreeable tasks, and to the inclemency of the weather; and finally use intoxicants very rarely and sparingly, or, better still, abstain from them altogether until you are twenty-one years old.

3. Use the supernatural means of grace, without which no virtue can long endure. Say your morning and evening prayers regularly; cultivate a special devotion to the Blessed Virgin Mary, saying three Hail Mary's for purity every morning and evening; go to Holy Communion every week or even daily, if possible, and to Confession every two weeks, seeking your confessor's instructions and advice in all doubts and temptations.

Instruction 7

My dear Daughter,

Perhaps you can recall how delighted you were when, as a little girl in school, you heard for the first time of the beauties and joys of Paradise, the original home of Adam and Eve. And many a time since, no doubt, you have found yourself thinking how lovely it must have been in the garden of Eden, and how sad it is that that wonderful home was lost to us by sin.

It is good to think such thoughts, because they remind us how good God is, and what a terrible thing sin is. God wanted us all to live in Paradise. He created man to be happy even here on earth. And what a glorious life He had planned for us and actually gave to our First Parents! There was neither heat nor cold; no rain, no snow, no storms or blustery winds, but always blue skies and pleasant sunshine and gentle breezes. There was neither sickness nor pain nor death; not even weariness or fatigue, but uninterrupted enjoyment of well-being and happiness.

But then came sin; Adam and Eve ate of the forbidden fruit, and all was changed. Storm clouds hid the cheerful face of heaven; roses grew thorns; the earth yielded weeds, poisonous plants and thistles; animals ran wild, throwing off the yoke of submission to man; the entire earth became a rebellious kingdom that had to be conquered and reclaimed. And poor man, man who had been the lord of creation, now found himself a dethroned king, in fear of the very creatures that erstwhile had done his every bidding, and faced by the open rebellion of the passions of his own heart.

This last circumstance was the saddest of all the visible results of the fall of man, because it indicated the loss of his supernatural gifts, especially the gifts of innocence and integrity.

You know, my dear child, that Adam and Eve had no need of clothing in Paradise. Holy Scripture says: "And they both were naked; to wit, Adam and his wife, and were not ashamed" (Gen. 2:25). The reason why they were not ashamed was that God had given them a special gift, called integrity or original innocence. Their bodies were just the same as ours exteriorly, but, by reason of this gift of integrity, their bodies were entirely subject to their souls, and all their passions and desires and animal appetites were obedient to their reason and their will.

This was, however, an extraordinary gift and dependent on Adam's keeping the commandment to abstain from the forbidden fruit. Hence no sooner had he eaten that fruit than he lost the gift of integrity, and in consequence he felt in his body the unruly stirring of his passions and was ashamed.

I think I can make the cause of this feeling of shame still clearer to you if I call your attention to man's twofold nature. Man, as you know, *i.e.*, a human being, whether man or woman, is made up of body and soul; he is partly animal and partly spiritual. Our body has the inclinations, feelings, and appetites of an animal. It craves food and drink and whatever gratifies the senses, and likes to lie at ease or to shout and play. Our soul, however, has altogether different desires. It loves spiritual things. It likes to think, to reason, to study, to acquire knowledge, to plan great things, and to prove the superiority of spirit over matter by using material things to express the ideas of the mind, as we see in the works of architecture, sculpture, painting and music, and in all the various inventions.

Now, when God put these two different natures together to form human nature in Adam and Eve, He most graciously added the gift of integrity in order to restrain all their animal appetites and subdue them to the control of their will. Their animal nature was, in consequence, just like a tame animal that is trained to obey every command of its master. All their animal cravings, passions, and impulses were, as it were, dormant or asleep, and became active only when and as far as bidden by their sovereign will.

Just imagine, then, my dear, that you had a nature like that:—that you would never feel any inclination to eat or drink more than was good for you; never would be inclined to laziness or anger; in fact, never would be inclined to indulge any of your animal appetites until your will had given the command to do so. And then imagine that all of a sudden, not only without the consent of your will but even against the resistance of your will, all these lower animal cravings would become active in you, and you would feel them tugging, as it were, at your will and trying to force it to yield to these unruly desires. That is precisely what happened to Adam and Eve when they lost the gift of integrity. Feeling for the very first time the rebellion of their flesh against their spirit; and realizing that this revolt of their lower nature was apparent to each other, they felt deeply humiliated and sore ashamed, and, hastening to sew together fig leaves, they made themselves aprons to conceal their nakedness.

This Scriptural account of the fall of Adam and Eve explains very clearly why the sense of shame is common to all human beings who have the use of reason. It is simply the natural result of the rebellion of the flesh against the spirit. The sight of the naked body instinctively makes us aware of this humiliating fact, and it is only natural that we should wish to hide our rebellious flesh and feel embarrassed if it is exposed.

The virtue that regulates one's conduct in regard to this feeling of shame is the virtue of modesty. Disregard of the dictates of this sense of shame is called immodesty; and excessive or merely affected regard for it is called prudery. As a rule, in the presence of others, modesty requires that the entire body be covered, with the exception of the head, the forearms, the hands and feet, which are regarded as the most dignified members of the body. Such is also the usual manner of dress among civilized nations. The upper arms, the legs (especially from the knees up), the back and breast are called by moralists the less seemly parts, which ought not be exposed except for a good reason.

Original sin, therefore, or Adam's fall from a state of innocence, and not merely the inclemency of the weather, was the reason why it became necessary from that time on for people to wear clothing. With the two exceptions of our dear Lord and His Blessed Mother, both of whom possessed the gift of integrity, all of Adam's descendants inherited Adam's nature as it was corrupted by his fall. Hence, our animal passions, which before Adam's fall were like perfectly tame animals, are now like animals that can be held in subjection only by being kept in chains. And keeping our bodies properly covered is one of the most important natural means of keeping our animal passions under control.

This is especially true of that passion or appetite by which persons of one sex are attracted to person of the opposite sex. God could, if He chose, have peopled the earth with only men or only women. But He chose to create both; and He chose also, with the sole exception of our Lord Himself, to make use of a man and a woman whenever He wished to create other human beings after Adam and Eve. As the union of a man and a woman in marriage is a means chosen by the infinite wisdom of God for increasing the number of men on earth and the future inhabitants of heaven, He made man so that persons of one sex have a natural attraction for persons of the other sex, and are thus drawn towards each other and led to enter the state of matrimony.

This mutual attraction between persons of opposite sex is called sex attraction or sex appeal; and as its purpose is to lead to marriage, it does not ordinarily make itself felt until boys and girls are of marriageable age. Yet, though it exists in all normal men and women, it is not so strong that it cannot be withstood or also counterbalanced by other attractions; and hence we find that many men and women prefer the single to the married state. Some, like bachelors and bachelor girls, remain single because they prefer the greater freedom and lesser responsibility of the single state. Others, like priests and nuns, do so in order to give themselves entirely to Jesus and to obtain the greater reward that our Lord promised to those who embrace the state of virginity out of love for Him.

Now that you know of the existence of this sex attraction, you will be able to understand better why it is so important for women to be very careful to observe modesty of dress. Our animal appetites or desires are aroused by the sight of the things they crave. Thus our appetite for food is aroused by the sight of something good to eat, and we say it makes our mouth water. So it is, too, with the sex appetite; it is aroused by the mere sight of the object of its desire. Yet, though it exists in both sexes, it is by nature stronger in men than in women; for God made men more responsive to sex appeal than women so that they would be impelled to seek a mate. And on the other hand, as God gave women an instinctive desire to be sought by men, He also gave them an inborn sense of modesty and reserve to act as a check for their own protection. This explains why a man's sex appetite is more easily aroused than a woman's, and why man courts the woman and not the woman the man. It explains also why women must be more careful than men to conceal their form and their person in order not unduly to tax men's power of controlling their sex appetite. It is quite true that men are obliged to control themselves and not do entertain impure desires or even to indulge their passion by kisses and embraces; but so are women obliged not to give the men unnecessary provocation. If it is true, as Christ Himself says, that "whosoever shall look on a woman to lust after her, hath already committed adultery with her in his heart," then those women are certainly not without sin who wear such scanty or clinging garments that they shamelessly expose their flesh or their form and thereby stir up and inflame in men these unholy desires.

Instruction 8

My dear Daughter,

From what you learned about purity in Catechism class, you know that it requires one to avoid certain looks and touches on oneself and on others. In other words, purity requires one to show proper reverence for one's own body as well as for the bodies of others. From the fact that sinful looks at oneself or others, and sinful touches or exposure of the body, are commonly called immodest looks, touches, and exposure, many people conclude that certain parts of the body must be immodest. Such a conclusion is just as false as to conclude that wine must be something evil because it can be instrumental in causing the evil of drunkenness. Just as it is not the wine that is evil but the immoderate use of it, so no parts of the body are immodest but only the abuse of them.

God created the human body to be a temple of the Holy Ghost; and when our souls are in the state of sanctifying grace, God actually resides within us as in a consecrated temple. And as our soul is in every part of our body, every part of our body belongs to this temple, every part is dwelt in by God, is sacred and holy and deserving of our reverence. This is true also of those parts which purity requires you to keep hidden, and which for that reason are called the private parts. They are the parts that are different in men and women, and, in fact, the parts that determine the sex of a human being, making one either a man or a woman, a boy or a girl. Even these parts, I say, are perfectly pure and sacred and deserving of reverence.

In Latin they are even called "the parts to be reverenced"; and by placing them hidden away as it were in the hollow of your lap, God Himself has indicated that they are of a more delicate nature than your other exterior organs. By covering them, too, with a natural drapery of soft hair, God plainly shows that He wished them to be modestly curtained even from your own eyes.

But if these parts are not immodest, why must you cover them? Why all this secrecy about them? One reason is the very sacredness of this part of your body as the portal of the temple of human life. As the gateway through which new human lives enter into this world, that part of a woman's body is truly sacred and should be most carefully guarded by the stern sentinels of privacy and modesty. The other reason I have already told you; namely, because the sight of these parts is likely to arouse the desire for sexual pleasures, which are most strictly reserved by Almighty God exclusively to the holy state of Matrimony. It is these two truths revealed by God, namely, the sacredness of the body as the living temple of the Holy Ghost, and the concupiscence of the body resulting from original sin, which constitute the twofold and ever existing reason for the practice of modesty. The pagan practice of disregarding these truths by frank exposure of the nude body, especially in the presence of relatives and intimate friends, has become so common that it has invaded even some Catholic circles and Catholic homes. But you must know, my dear child, that there is no excuse for such a practice among Christians. Hence, while dressing or undressing, not only in the presence of strangers but also in the presence of your sisters and mother, you should avoid exposing yourself from the knees to the shoulders. If modern pagans in their ignorance call that prudery, you will know that it is the supernatural virtue of Christian modesty.

Since the enjoyment of sexual pleasure is permissible only in the married state, and even there only under very definite restrictions, the willful indulgence in it outside the married state or in defiance of those restrictions, is always a mortal sin of impurity, not because there is anything impure or shameful in the pleasure itself, but because it is something shameful and impure to consent to it or to enjoy it against the will of God when one is not entitled to it.

There is nothing at all strange about this distinction because we make a similar distinction in regard to the enjoyment of other pleasures. Thus while you may enjoy a chicken dinner on Thursday, you are forbidden under mortal sin to do so on a Friday; and though to take a full meal ordinarily is something quite innocent in itself, it is forbidden to those who are about to receive Holy Communion. Then we make a distinction also between the moderate and the immoderate enjoyment of eating and drinking. To use food and drink for the purpose which God intended them and in the manner He intended is something good. To use them contrary to God's will is a sin.

Now, just as the pleasures of eating may be lawfully enjoyed only when they are indulged in in such a way as to achieve the purpose for which God intended food to be eaten, so the pleasures of sex may be lawfully enjoyed only when they are indulged in in such a manner so to achieve the purposes for which God intended them; namely, the purposes of the married state, the chief one of which is to increase the number of men on earth and of the saints of God in heaven.

Both gluttony and drunkenness are shameful vices, but impurity is even more so. The glutton and the drunkard have a right to at least some of the pleasures of eating and drinking; namely, to the moderate enjoyment of food and drink. They sin by going to excess. But an unmarried person has no right whatever to enjoy even the slightest sexual pleasure. Hence, if he nevertheless indulges in it, he usurps an exclusive right of the married state, just as truly as a layman would usurp a right of the priesthood if he went into a confessional and heard Confessions, or went to the altar and distributed Holy Communion.

This being true, sexual pleasures must remain a closed book to you so long as you are not married; and the only safe and sensible thing for you to do in the meantime is to put all thought and all curiosity regarding them as far as possible out of your mind. You know what terrible consequences followed from mother Eve's curiosity about the forbidden fruit; so be careful not to make a similar blunder. *So long as you are not married, sexual pleasure is for you forbidden fruit.* Yet as Almighty God, in commanding Adam and Eve not to eat of the fruit of a certain tree, did not leave them in ignorance but told them distinctly where the tree stood; so it may be well to inform you also that sexual pleasure, which is forbidden fruit to the unmarried, consists of certain pleasurable sensations that are felt in the sexual organs during the marital embrace.

Now that you know in what part of your body these sensations occur, you will know that you must never yield or consent to them, if you should ever experience them either from exciting dreams at night or from other involuntary causes during waking hours. You may be quite sure that the devil will be jealous of your innocence, and that as he came to Eve to deceive and seduce her by saying: "No, you shall not die. Your eyes shall be opened and you shall be like God," so he will also come to you to excite your curiosity and your desire for that forbidden fruit. But as soon as you notice the first promptings of such a temptation, outwit the devil by saying to yourself: "No, No! That is forbidden fruit! I don't want my eyes opened. Jesus and Mary, help me lest I do a wicked thing and sin against my God."

Whatever touches are necessary for health or cleanliness may be made without hesitation. But beyond that, the more strictly you observe the rule "Hands off," the better it will be for you. Do not think because you do not see what harm there can be in such touches, that there is no danger. You do not act thus in regard to physical dangers. Even though you may not understand what harm there can be in handling dynamite or such an innocent-looking think as nitroglycerine, you heed the warning of others and do not fool with them. Yet be assured, my child, that the physical harm that you might do to yourself by fooling with high explosives is nothing compared with the moral damage that may result to your soul from meddling with the private parts of your body. Therefore, whenever you bathe or are engaged in any way in the care of your body, bear in mind that your body is a temple of the Holy Ghost, and treat it with the reverence that a consecrated temple deserves. Remember, too, that your

Guardian Angel sees everything that you do, and ask him to guard you from ever doing anything against holy purity; for your own efforts will avail you little if you do not implore the grace of God.

Part Three

To be discussed with young women ages 14-16

NOTE ON THE NEXT INSTRUCTION

In the following instructions the parent should nowhere declare or imply that all unescorted activities among teenagers are sinful either in themselves or because they are in all cases bound up with the immediate danger of sexual sin.

What is said here is put as it is to jog the parent awake to the dangers involved, and make it her aim to win the girl's willing cooperation toward avoiding all dangers rather than running any risks.

Instruction 9

My dear Daughter,

It is quite a long time since I read to you the first one of these instructions, and during that time you have been developing rapidly, both mentally and physically, so that you have now entered upon the first stage of young-lady-hood.

Yet, although you are now a young lady, it is important for you to remember that you are as yet a very, *very* young and unexperienced young lady. Young ladies, you know, range all the way from fourteen years to thirty and over; and since there is a vast difference between a girl of fourteen and one of eighteen, and again between one of seventeen or eighteen and one of twenty-five, so it follows naturally that there should also be a difference between the privileges accorded to young ladies of different ages and circumstances. The time of youth, to which young ladies belong, is a time of preparation for mature womanhood. And because this preparation is stretched out over a number of years, it would be folly to give a girl in her early teens the same freedom that is granted to a girl in her twenties. The younger girl is not yet prepared for so much freedom. She is not aware of, and above all she does not realize, the dangers of such freedom; and in consequence she would not make the right use of it.

That is why Almighty God has imposed on parents the solemn duty of guiding and guarding their children most carefully especially during the years of adolescence, *i.e.*, of young manhood and young womanhood. It would be much easier for parents to let their children do as they please, just as it would be much easier for a pastor or confessor to let his parishioners or penitents do as they please, and not be continually warning them against dangers and urging them to practice virtue. But just as a pastor is responsible for his people, so are parents responsible for their children; and they will have to render a strict account to God, if through their lack of watchfulness and their easy-going yielding to their children's desires, they are the cause that their children suffer harm.

You see, my dear, there are still many dangers to the welfare of your body, as well as your soul, of which you are unaware. And even if you have perhaps been told of them, you have at least never experienced them, and hence you cannot realize how great the danger is but must simply take the word of your father and me and of your spiritual director for it, and avoid those things which we know would prove harmful to you.

I have read you an instruction on the chief one of these dangers; namely, that which results from the so-called sex appeal or sex attraction. You will remember that I told you that God put this mutual attraction in men and women so that persons of one sex would be attracted to persons of the opposite sex, and they would thus be led to contract marriage at the proper time. That is the sole object and purpose of this attraction. God did not give men and women this attraction towards each other merely that they might enjoy each other's company. No; it was put in us to lead up to marriage; and, therefore, if a man or woman has absolutely no intention or no possibility of ever getting married, he or she does wrong to run the risk of arousing this sex attraction and becoming exposed to the proximate occasion of sin.

And this same risk of becoming exposed to grave danger of sin is incurred not only by those who never intend to or cannot marry, but also by those who do not intend to or cannot marry *within a reasonable period of time.* And the reason is this. Since this sex attraction is intended to lead to marriage, and after marriage to the marital embrace, and thus to bringing children into this world, if a girl is several years too young to marry and nevertheless begins to associate with individual boys, she runs great risk of falling prematurely in love and of then being led by her passionate attachment to permit impure liberties (often called "petting" or "necking") or even the marital embrace. Such things are not at all manifestations of true love, which aims to promote another's true welfare; they are rather the result of yielding to the physical promptings of sex appeal, or to state it bluntly, to the passion of lust. If you only keep in mind what a strong appeal any normal girl's physical attractions make to any normal boy, your head will not be turned by the fact that they show great interest in you; and you will not imagine that you must possess great personal charm. On the contrary, you should rather fear that the boys take to you rather than to other girls, because they think that you will be an easy mark and will readily permit the liberties they seek.

But even supposing, what is *very* improbable, that there would be no danger of your yielding to the boys' impure desires, you should avoid early dating in order not to expose them to the danger of falling in love with you. You have no right to use your feminine charms to attract young men merely to show your power or to enjoy their attentions or to have them show you a good time and then to drop them cold-bloodedly when you notice that their interest in you is serious. Many a young man has been driven to drink and other bad habits after a girl who led him on for the sake of a good time finally jilted him and broke his heart.

Even when you will be old enough to seek a partner for marriage, dating will be full of dangers. But if you take proper precautions and have constant recourse to prayer and the sacraments, you can confidently count on God's help and protection. This is by no means true, however, when boys and girls who are too young to marry rashly expose themselves to these dangers merely in order to have a good time. And in their case, the dangers are the harder to overcome on account of the weak condition of their undeveloped characters.

Instruction 10

My dear Daughter,

When I warned you against the dangers of premature company-keeping, I realized quite well that the thought would probably come to you: "But nearly all the high-school girls of my acquaintance are dating. Are they, then, all doing wrong?" They may not all have fallen into the sins to which they are exposing themselves, and charity requires us not to think evil of them; yet it is nevertheless true, even though they may not know it, that they are doing wrong to expose themselves to such dangers; and experience proves only too often that ignorance does not shield them from the sad consequences of not avoiding those occasions of sin. Please impress this truth indelibly on your mind, my child: *The fact that something is being done by the majority of people does not prove that it is right.* If we want to adopt as our standard what we see the majority of people doing, then there will soon be no religious or virtuous people left in the world.

You see, my dear child, this is not a Christian country in which we live. *More than half* the people of the United States do not belong to any church at all; many do not even believe that there is a God; and even among those who call themselves Christians there are many who do not believe that Jesus is God. So since a great many Americans are practically pagans; since they do not accept the teachings of the Catholic Church regarding purity and the sacredness of the marriage contract; and since they know nothing whatever about sanctifying grace and the terrible evil of losing it, it is not surprising that they do things that are dangerous to the welfare of their souls, and that they make little or nothing of sins which a Catholic knows to be mortal.

Suppose you did not know anything about the value of sanctifying grace and did not believe that there is a hell; would you hesitate long to commit a mortal sin if you got a lot of pleasure out of it and were in no danger of being caught? Well, there are thousands and millions of your fellow Americans who know nothing of sanctifying grace and do not believe in hell; and do you think that their conduct can be a safe guide for you to follow? But it is just the conduct of such people–of practical pagans and downright atheists that has gradually come to constitute the standard of morality adopted by a vast number of our countrymen.

And when Catholics go to see movies and plays, and read magazines and books in which the characters act according to this low moral standard, they, too, become contaminated by these false principles of morality. They gradually come to think that what so many people do cannot be so bad; and since we are all more prone to evil than to good, they easily try to persuade themselves that the Church is too strict, and that certain practices are not as bad as she makes them. And so it happens that, although these Catholics learned at school that they must avoid dangerous occasions of sin, they quiet their conscience by saying that certain improper dances, indecent shows, immodest styles, and dangerous intimacies between boys and girls may be indulged in because "everybody is doing it."

I know quite well that if certain girls were told that they are too young to have boyfriends, they would reply: "Well, can't a girl have any fun at all? Some people want to take all the joy out of life." But such a reply would be both foolish and unjust. Are girls so helpless that they cannot have any fun without boys? A girl should be ashamed to admit that. And I know it to be a fact that not only many girls under eighteen but even in their twenties have clubs which meet regularly at the home of one of the members, and they have a most delightful time without any boys present.

And as to the accusation that parents and priests and others who object to boys and girls dating at an early age, want to take all the joy out of life, nothing could be more unjust. The motive and object of such parents and priests is to guard the young folks' happiness by protecting them against their own imprudent desires. You know very well that a child often wants to have something, *e.g.*, a knife, a pistol, or certain food, which no one who loves the child would permit it to have, because it would only prove harmful to it. Now, the same is true also of boys and girls who are just entering manhood and womanhood. Anybody must admit that the parents of a girl of sixteen or seventeen have had more experience and know more about life's dangers than the girl herself; that is, supposing that the girl is a good girl and has not been permitted to run wild. And since such a good girl cannot reasonably question her parents' love for her and their wisdom in placing certain restrictions on her conduct, she ought to observe these restrictions gladly and thank Heaven that she has parents who do their duty and try to promote her real welfare and happiness.

In view of all these facts, my great love for you prompts me to give you the following advice in regard to your relations with boys; namely, to put all thought of courtship out of your mind until you are eighteen years old; that is, till you are old enough to think of marrying and of courting for the proper purpose of finding a suitable partner. That is the only way that you can succeed in guarding your heart from becoming entangled in one of those early love affairs which are so premature and so displeasing to sensible people that they are called by the contemptuous name of "puppy loves."

That does not mean that you must run away or cross the street in order not to meet a boy whom you spy at a distance. Neither does it mean that you must never, never meet any boys socially at home gatherings or parties in company with other boys and girls in the presence of your or their parents. What I mean is that there should be no pairing off of one boy with one girl; and that in going to and from such social gatherings a girl not of age should not have a boyfriend as her companion but a girl or her brother or parents. You can readily understand that there is infinitely more danger of a boy and a girl growing intimate, of exchanging endearments, and of falling in love when they are by themselves than when they are in a crowd. Hence you should not have any individual "dates" with boys; all invitations to go out with a boy, whether to a movie, a dance or party, a street-car or automobile ride, should not be accepted; and you should *on principle* and for safety's sake so guard your heart and its affections that you will not incur the risk of becoming entangled by any love affair before your eighteenth birthday.

If you have thus guarded your heart and strengthened your character by self-denial until you are really old enough to marry, then you can step out of your retirement like a queen and meet and associate with young men and be courted by them for the true purpose of courtship, namely, for the purpose of seeking a life mate with whom to establish a home and a family after the pattern of the Holy Family of Nazareth.

Many of your friends will no doubt call you old-fashioned and foolish, or perhaps even sneer at you, if you follow my advice in this matter. But you can afford to smile at, or rather pity, their ignorance and delusion; for you are better informed and wiser than they, and your course of conduct will bring you not only greater blessings but also greater and more lasting happiness in the end.

Instruction 11

My dear Daughter,

In the instruction on purity, I already called your attention to the reverence you owe to your body because it is a temple of the Holy Ghost. Ignorance or disregard of this sublime truth is undoubtedly one of the reasons why so many people think that they may use their body as they please without any regard for its dignity and sacred character. Added to this, as another cause of the deplorable lack of modesty in so many people, is ignorance or the denial of original sin and its consequences for soul and body.

It is true that the soul's white robe of sanctifying grace, which was lost by the sin of Adam, is restored in Baptism through the merits of the Precious Blood of our Blessed Redeemer. But the body's robe of innocence as well as its armor of immortality, which were both likewise lost by original sin, are not restored in this life. In consequence of this loss, just as it is necessary for man to guard his body by clothing against the danger of death and the ravages of disease, so it is also necessary for him to cover his body and its members in order that his gaze may not fall on objects that stir up his passions and he become a prey to his own body's unruly animal desires.

Now, these two facts, the dignity of the body as a temple of the Holy Ghost and the concupiscence or inordinate animal cravings of the body which resulted from original sin, demand the observance of certain precautions in regard to the body both in our own private conduct as well as in our relations with others. As I have already warned you how to conduct yourself in the care you must needs extend to your body, I shall now explain how you should act in your dealings and associations with others, in particular those with whom the dangers are greatest and most frequent, namely, with persons of the opposite sex.

Although as intelligent beings, we can communicate with one another, *e.g.*, by signs and speech and by writing, without any bodily contact and even without any close proximity, still, as beings that have a body as well a soul, we very naturally crave the company of persons of flesh and blood like ourselves; and the more common our interests, the more intimate our relations and the greater our mutual affection, the closer and the more intimate we like also our bodies to be. This is not only natural but also proper; and the practice of cultured and virtuous people proves it to be a fact. And what is more, the practice of self-respecting people in this point is based on those two truths I have just pointed out; namely, the reverence which the body deserves as a temple of God, and the reserve to be exercised in regard to bodily contacts that may tend to stir up concupiscence.

This will become much clearer to you when I proceed to details. Is there not a vast difference between the distance at which you keep perfect strangers, passing acquaintances, distant relatives, and ordinary friends; and close friends, close relatives, and the immediate members of your family? You would not walk arm in arm with a girl with whom you have only a speaking acquaintance. Still less would you and she be seen walking along with an arm around each other's waist. Those are bodily contacts reserved for close friends. A lady does not even extend her hand in greeting when she is introduced to a gentleman by a common friend. And if she is a real lady, no gentleman who is not closely related to her will receive the salutation of her lips.

So you see, my dear child, how the practice of respectable people draws a sharp line of distinction between the physical tokens of regard that they bestow upon persons with whom they come in social contact. Some they greet with a nod; to some they offer their hand; to others they may give an arm; but only to intimate friends and relatives, their cheek or lips. And the reason is that in all these tokens of love and esteem there are greater or lesser degrees of sacredness, which would be entirely eliminated if the more intimate endearments were bestowed indiscriminately upon all.

Above all, kisses and embraces should be regarded as something very sacred; and no girl who is free with her kisses can safely be predicted as one who will make an ideal wife and mother. She shows herself too flighty, too cheap. If she herself sets so little value on her lips and cheeks that she readily yields them to different boys, then she will be very apt to permit also other liberties that will soon lower her self-esteem still further and in the end destroy her virtue. But when a girl has led such a life before marriage, there is danger that she will not be content with the love of one man after she becomes a wife and mother.

From this you can conclude what is to be thought of those parties where so-called kissing games are played, and where the sacred character of the kiss is degraded, cheapened, and coarsened, by being imposed as a penalty in games of chance. If you ever think of yourself as a future bride, is the boy you picture as your ideal husband a boy who has bestowed his kisses on numerous other girls? Or is he not rather a boy who has held his lips in reserve for the girl of his dreams—the girl who promised to become his wife and the mother of his children? But if you would like a husband who had saved his kisses for you, do you not think it proper that you should also hold your lips in reserve for him?

Believe me, my dear child, this levity and reckless abandon with which so many young people treat the matter of kissing and caressing, is one of the chief causes that lead them to indulge in downright impure liberties with each other and even into the terrible sin of arrogating to themselves while still single the sacred privileges of the married state. Yes, some unmarried young people even perform the marital act together; and if the girl becomes a mother in consequence, in very many cases, to hide her sin she adds the sin of murder to that of impurity by mercilessly killing the helpless babe in her womb.

These are terrible things, my child—sins in fact that cry to Heaven for vengeance; but they are the natural consequences of that utterly pagan custom of our day of allowing mere boys and girls to date as if they were of marriageable age; and not only that, but of according them practically as much privacy in their associations with each other as if they were actually married. And, from living side by side with people who have these low moral standards, many Catholics who know better or certainly should know better are also led astray and fall into these awful sins.

It is hard to explain, but it is a fact that Catholics are sometimes worse than non-Catholics in this respect, and that non-Catholics girls sometimes have higher standards than Catholic ones. Just listen to what the conductor of the woman's department in a non-Catholic daily paper says on this subject in reply to a letter from a girl names Susie:

A boy told Susie, she is the kind of a girl that men forget, and Susie is broken-hearted over the remark. She says she is pretty, a fashionable dresser, that she kisses the boys any time they ask her and can't see anything wrong in it in spite of what old fogies say. She can go to a party and drink beer, smoke cigarettes, and never forget herself. She doesn't mind if the men do "neck," because she can tell them where to get off before they to go too far.

Wonder if Susie herself has not given a pretty fair picture of the kind of girl men forget. Let's look at this girl you've presented here, Susie. How would you sum her up? Isn't cheap the word? Isn't the cheap girl the one men forget–because there isn't anything about her worth remembering? Men do not forget the girl who puts enough value on herself to repulse their too familiar advances. They do not forget the girl who knows you cannot demand respect by words when your conduct belies them. In her they brush up against something clean and fine that leaves an impress. The girl men don't forget, Susie, is the one who reminds them of the better stuff they're made of. The cheap girl doesn't. That's why they forget her.

So there you have the conductor of a department in a secular daily paper setting down the girl who is free with her kisses as the cheap girl–the kind that men forget. And listen to what another woman column-writer in a non-

Catholic daily says: "By throwing away your favors, girls, by letting all sort of boys kiss you and hold you in their arms, you really do spoil marriage. You never can go back, never can know the fresh sweetness of belonging to one person; the pride of being all purity and trust and kindness for that one alone."

But how can you refrain from giving a kiss if it is imposed as a penalty at a party you attend with other Catholic girls and boys of your age? Simply by refusing to do so. Let it be known right at the start that you will not take part in any kissing games nor execute any penalty that involves kissing. And if you thus show that you have courage enough to dare to be different, and explain the reason for your stand, the better class of your girl friends will probably follow your example and content themselves with games more suited to self-respecting young ladies and gentlemen. And even supposing you should run into such a kissing penalty entirely unexpectedly by surprise, who can make you carry it out? Are your companions not young ladies and gentlemen? If so, how can they compel you to kiss a boy? But if they are not *ladies and gentlemen*, then turn your back on them, put on your hat and coat, and go home. The idea of anybody being able to make you kiss a boy against your will!

I must call your attention to one more point and then I will bring this long instruction to a close. I spoke before of kissing leading do downright impure liberties. A girl would be guilty of permitting such liberties if she allowed touches on her breasts, on her limbs or body close to the private parts, and of course on the private parts themselves. All such deliberate touches are mortal sins; and so too, are all actions (kisses included) that are indulged in with sexual pleasure; because, as I explained in a former instruction, the enjoyment of that pleasure is most strictly restricted by Almighty God exclusively to the holy state of Matrimony.

It is true, of course, that not every kiss between a boy and a girl is always and necessarily a sin. There may be light and hasty kisses indulged in by thoughtless young folks that are not sinful; but the step from such kisses to venially sinful kisses is very swift. And when kisses become eager, ardent, and often repeated or long drawn out, they are practically always mortal sins, because they naturally arouse sexual passion—if not in the girl, at least in the boy.

You know from your catechism that you are obliged to avoid dangerous occasions of sin; but you probably did not know till now how much danger lies in actions so commonly looked upon and represented on stage and screen as harmless tokens of endearment. Hereafter, therefore, if anyone tries to convince you that kissing, embracing, fondly holding hands, and similar actions between unmarried persons of opposite sex are perfectly innocent and legitimate pastime, you will know better and you will doubtless also thank God that you were warned in time. As knowledge alone, however, will not save you when you are tempted by the enticements of the flesh, continue to strengthen yourself by the devout recital of the three Hail Mary's for purity at your morning and evening prayer and by the frequent reception of the Sacraments.

Instruction 12

My dear Daughter,

In the last instruction that I gave you (quite a long time ago), I explained to you that, as the purpose of courtship is to find a suitable partner with whom to enter the holy state of Matrimony, boys and girls should not begin to court until they are of marriageable age. Since today is your eighteenth birthday and your are now of marriageable age, the time is very opportune for me to give you some advice as to what you should do and what you should avoid during this romantic period of your life.

In order to get the correct view of courtship and to take the proper attitude toward it right from the start, it is necessary to bear in mind that the time of courtship is *not a state of life* but a period of transition; and that falling in love is not to be engaged in for its own sake or for the sake of the pleasure it affords, but as a preparation for the state of Matrimony. Hence if a girl has decided to enter the convent, she should not begin to court at all.

There is no denying the fact that for the average girl whose vocation is the married state, the time of courtship holds some of the sweetest joys of life. But these very joys themselves point to marriage as their culmination, for back of the lovers' present enjoyment of each other is always the thought and the hope that their present all too brief hours of companionship will one day be crowned by a life-long inseparable union in the home of their dreams.

But if the time of courtship is a time of preparation for marriage, it follows necessarily that when a girl enters that stage of her life, she should give serious thought to the obligations which the married state involves. Many a girl looks upon the day of her coming of age merely as the day of her emancipation from the restrictions of girlhood and of her entry upon a period of absolute independence. Such a view is not only wrong but dangerous as well. A girl who is of age may not simply do as she pleases–go and come as she pleases–but still owes her parents not only love and reverence but also obedience as long as she remains under the parental roof. Prudent parents will, of course, gradually grant her a considerable amount of independence in order to accustom her to decide and act for herself, but they are still responsible for her and should gently yet firmly use their parental authority to shield her from forming dangerous habits and companionships.

The reason why you should now give serious thought to the obligations of marriage is because if you do not do so before you fall in love, you will not be likely to do so afterwards. The fact is that the mentality of a girl in love usually admits of no serious reflection on the sterner things of life, and in consequence sees no need of preparation for the duties of married life. All the more reason, then, for you to do some serious thinking now. What would you think of a young man who would want to be ordained priest without having seriously contemplated the obligations of the priesthood, and without having striven to fit himself for the proper performance of his duties as a priest? But the candidate for the married state also faces most serious and difficult obligations–to himself, to his partner in marriage, to his children, to God and to the Church, to his country and to society at large; and it would be folly for any one to expect to fulfill all these obligations without having prepared himself for them beforehand.

Now, the first thing, my dear child, that a girl contemplating marriage should bear in mind is that the familiar fairy tale ending "And they lived happy ever after" does not represent the actual course of marriage in real life. Marriage means crosses and sacrifices, anxieties and disappointments, labor and suffering, just the same as the priesthood and the religious state. And only they who are willing and unselfish enough to sacrifice their own ease and comfort for the designs of God and the good of others in Matrimony, will achieve success and find true peace and happiness in that state.

What the designs of God are in regard to Matrimony are expressed very aptly by the two terms "Matrimony" and "conjugal state." Matrimony, from the Latin words "*matris munium*," means "office of mother"; and the office of mother is none other than the office of bearing and rearing children. You see, then, how wrong it would be to enter the married state with the intention of shirking the very purpose and office of Matrimony in order to continue to lead a life of ease and pleasure and personal independence as before. To do that would be just as wrong as for a man to enter the priesthood and assume the office of pastor and then to shirk the duties of his office by refusing to preach, to say Mass, to hear Confessions, and to visit the sick.

The word "conjugal" comes from the Latin word "*conjugium*" which means a joining together by a yoke. A yoke, you know, is not a decoration like the bridal wreath, but something binding two together for a common work. The conjugal state, therefore, is the state of a man and a woman who have assumed together the yoke of obligation of laboring together to achieve the purpose of the married state: namely, the rearing of a family.

It is evident, then, that marriage is not a sinecure but a serious vocation. But that is also the beautiful thing about Matrimony, just the same as about the priesthood, that its reward as far as it is realized here below, comes precisely from the unselfish performance of its obligations. Or what do you think is the greatest earthly happiness that comes to the girl who enters the married state? What is the greatest thrill of her life? Is it that moment, so sung in story, when her beloved prince charming elicits her promise to become his bride and presses the first sacred kiss on her chaste maiden lips? No, my child. Is it perhaps that long desired moment when, with wedding bells aringing, and amid the organ's trembling tones, she accepts her fiancé's pledge of fidelity "till death do us part"? Again I say, No, my child. Neither is it the pleasure attending the marital embrace by which marriage is consummated and the marriage tie made indissoluble. For, although in that embrace husband and wife become so completely one that, as the Bible expresses it, they become "two in one flesh," still it is not in that act itself but in the result that God intended to produce through it that a Christian wife finds her greatest joy.

Yes, dear, the supreme thrill that comes to the happily wedded wife is that which fills her soul when she clasps her first-born to her mother's breast and sees in it not only the joint product of its parents' love, but also the union of their own very substance into a new being, in which each can trace the beloved features of the other, and which will exist forever as a monument of their love.

Add to this the mother's further happy thought that by the assiduous performance of her maternal duties, by her prayers, her instructions, her wise counsels, training and good examples, she can mold this child into a beautiful character that will be a joy to men and angels and give glory to God for all eternity, you will understand clearly how true it is that the most worthwhile and lasting joys of wedded life come from the unselfish fulfillment of the sacred office of motherhood. That is the reason, too, why our Blessed Savior Himself said: "When a woman hath brought forth a child, she remembereth no more the anguish [of childbirth] for joy that a man is born into this world" (Jn. 16:21).

Only if you view marriage in this light, will you be likely to escape those moral pitfalls which so often prove disastrous to girls who are keeping company. For, viewing marriage as a serious matter, you will also regard courtship, which leads to marriage, as a serious matter; and in weighing the qualifications of the young men you meet, you will judge of their fitness for your companionship and for your hand not by their ability to offer you a good time but by their ability to bear the yoke of wedded life and to fulfill the duties of father to your children.

Fortified with this serious outlook on courtship, you will not allow it to degenerate into a dangerous though pleasurable pastime. And realizing that the kissing and embracing so often indulged in during this period may easily become a serious occasion of sin (even more so to the boy than to the girl), you will not permit it until you are engaged, and then only sparingly and with great caution. There will be little danger of your failing in this regard if you receive your gentlemen friends at home with other members of the family present, which is the proper and Christian way to entertain your friends. Every boy and girl whose intentions are honorable will welcome the presence of others as a safeguard against their own weakness and as a proof of the innocence of their relations. To say that there is no danger in their being alone together is like saying that you may put straw and live coals together without danger of fire. The custom of chaperonage, therefore, is dictated not only by Christian prudence but also by plain common sense; and the practice, so pernicious in its results yet so common nowadays, of according young couples almost as much privacy and seclusion as if they were married, is condemned even by decent pagans.

It is idle to say that the boy and the girl should pray and receive the Sacraments often and remember their dignity, and then there will be no danger if they are alone together. "He that loveth danger will perish in it!" Their first duty is to *avoid* the danger; and when that is impossible, they must use both natural and supernatural means to pass through it unharmed. Should you, therefore, at any time happen to be alone with a young man, you should give him clearly to understand more by your deportment than by words that he must keep his hands off your person. And do not make the terrible mistake of thinking that because *your* passions are not aroused by certain contacts, there is no danger for the young man either. Just because God intended that the man should court the woman and not the woman the man, He gave man a nature far more responsive to sex appeal than that of a woman. And because in the relations between the sexes man is the aggressive party, God gave woman an innate sense of modesty, coyness, and timid reserve for her own protection. It is only on the supposition of a girl's utter ignorance of this difference in the sexes that I can understand how a girl can sit on a boy's lap and then be surprised or even indignant when he regards her action as an invitation to take liberties.

Most of your girl friends would perhaps laugh at the cautions here given; but by observing them, my child, you will not only spare yourself many a pang of conscience but you will also preserve the physical endearments of love in all their freshness for your married life, when they can be indulged in their proper purpose of easing the burdens of wedded life, cementing more firmly the marriage union, and keeping alive some of the romance of love long after the days of courtship are over.

Having devoted the greater part of this instruction to impressing upon you the serious nature of marriage and courtship, let me in conclusion help you to realize the sacred character of the marriage act. You will no doubt remember that in a previous instruction I stated that the Sacrament of Holy Matrimony, like the Sacrament of Holy Orders, gives rights and privileges as well as obligations and powers not enjoyed by those who have not received this Sacrament. Now, the great privilege of married couples is to co-operate with Almighty God in bringing new intelligent beings into existence, just as it is the privilege of the priest to co-operate with God in bringing Jesus Christ upon our altars. To bring an immortal being into existence is so solemn an act that when God created the first man, He did not simply say "Let man be made," but calling upon the other two persons of the Blessed Trinity, He said: "Let us make man." Then, having formed a human body out of the earth, He breathed into it an immortal soul, and man became a living image and likeness of God Himself.

What a distinction it would have been for the great sculptor Michelangelo if God had said to him: "Come, let us make a living statue of Myself. I will direct how to make it out of your own materials and with your own instruments; and then I will breathe into it an immortal soul and it will exist forever as the joint product of your skill and My power."

Such a distinction is actually granted by Almighty God to all parents. In His infinite wisdom God placed the instruments and the materials for making an image of Himself in the parents' own bodies, fashioning the latter in such a way that in the marital embrace the husband's generative organ fits into that of the wife. And in His infinite love, God ordained that as a climax to that loving embrace, a precious substance containing the germ of life is transmitted from husband to wife to be united with a similar substance in her womb for the formation of a tiny human body. In the very same instant that those two elements, the father cell and the mother cell, unite in an eternal embrace to form a body, God creates in it an immortal soul, thus making a living image of Himself, an indestructible link between husband and wife, and an everlasting memorial of their mutual love.

And thus you see, my dear child, what a wonderful and sacred act the marital embrace is, and what an intimate union God has established through it between your dear father and me and yourself.